Military Aircraft Library
Ground Attack Planes

Military Aircraft Library
Ground Attack Planes

DR. DAVID BAKER

Rourke Enterprises, Inc.
Vero Beach, FL 32964

16172

Library of Congress Cataloging-in-Publication Data

Baker, David, 1944-
  Ground attack planes/by David Baker.

  p. cm. — (The Military aircraft series)
  Includes index.
  Summary: Describes different types of military ground attack planes and their uses at various times in history.
  ISBN 0-86592-536-4
  1. Attack planes — Juvenile literature 2. Attack planes — United States — Juvenile literature. 3. Fighter planes — Juvenile literature. 4. Fighter planes — United States — Juvenile Literature. 5. Close air support — Juvenile literature. [1. Attack planes. 2. Airplanes, Military. 3. Close air support.]
I. Title. II. Series: Baker, David, 1944-   Military aircraft Library.
UG1242.A28B35   1989   88-34071
358.4'3 — dc19
                                    CIP
                                    AC

CONTENTS

The Mission

Modern airplanes designed for aggressive duty in war fall into three distinct categories: fighters, bombers, and ground attack planes. Fighters include *interceptors* that fly out to meet and attack intruding enemy planes and aircraft designed to protect other planes on special missions. Bombers are designed to fly great distances and hit targets deep behind enemy lines. Ground attack planes are built to hit ground forces and help friendly armies win battles.

When aircraft are used for unusual duties, the divisions between the three can get blurred. In addition, there are other categories that support military operations in wartime. These include reconnaissance planes, cargo planes, troop transport planes, airborne tankers to refuel fighters, attack planes, and many others. Sometimes the defined duties of individual categories also overlap.

One of the best ground attack planes of World War Two was the British Typhoon.

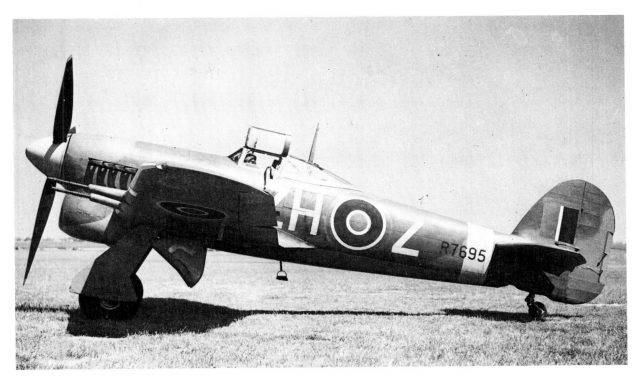

The Typhoon was equipped with guns and could carry rockets or bombs for strikes on ground targets.

In World War Two (1939-45), British bombers were being used to pound German cities and to destroy factories and production lines making weapons. A great debate arose when the bombers were ordered to support the invasion of mainland Europe in June 1944. Since 1940, the Germans had controlled the whole of Western Europe, and American and British forces were planning a great invasion. They would be supported by many other countries, including Canada, Australia, New Zealand, and India.

The bombers were taken away from their principal role and used instead to hit German positions on the coast of France, clearing the way for invasion. Although they were being used in a ground attack role, they were far from being ground attack planes. In other examples, heavy fighters are sometimes converted into strike planes. When jets came along in the 1950s and

nuclear weapons were invented, a single fighter could hit a city behind enemy lines with more explosive power than all the bombs dropped in World War Two. Yet it was not a bomber.

The best example of an airplane used in a true ground attack role occurred when the Nazi German air force developed the *blitzkrieg* concept of surprise attack. *Blitzkrieg* is the German word for lightning war, an appropriate word when applied to the methods used by German forces in 1939 to invade Poland. Using a terrifying dive bomber, the Stuka, in conjunction with a massive, high-speed ground assault, the Nazi troops raced through Poland without stopping.

Each Stuka, or Junkers Ju-87, was built as a dive bomber with a siren that sent out a high-pitched wailing sound as air rushed through it. The screaming sound of a Stuka diving almost vertically down toward the ground is a sound no

Modern fighters carry out a variety of different roles; this Phantom can be used as a fighter or a strike plane.

As a strike aircraft, the F-4 Phantom has seen wide service with many air forces.

Even a lightweight interceptor like the General Dynamics F-16 has many different roles to play.

one who experienced it would ever forget. Releasing its bombs from low level, the Stuka pulled out just in time to prevent the plane crashing to the ground.

It was not long before Stuka dive bombers were used to attack cities, military installations, and many targets where accurate bombing was not as essential as the sheer panic the Stukas' presence could cause among civilians. Not that they were inaccurate. Because they flew so low before releasing their bombs, and because they were flown literally pointing their noses at the target, there was very little error in sending the bombs to their intended destinations. The Stuka has forever remained the classic horror weapon of terror bombing on civilians and refugees.

Later in the war the Germans developed a very effective anti-tank plane. Built by Henschel and

9

known as the Hs 129, one version carried an enormous 75mm cannon in addition to a wide variety of machine guns and anti-armor weapons. The German air force pressed this type of plane into service because it was the only type of weapon that could deal effectively with the big Russian tanks that were facing German forces on the ground.

The Germans learned the value of ground attack early in the war by using dive bombers to make lightning assaults. When they were themselves pressed by massed columns of armor, they realized how important air power over the battlefield was to the outcome of a war. Planes like the American Republic P-51 Thunderbolt and the British Hawker Typhoon were used with blistering effect on retreating German army units, smashing up armor, tanks, and field guns without challenge.

After World War Two, the use of aircraft to influence ground activity was extended. The availability of small, tactical, nuclear weapons

Two Sidewinder missiles, a 2,000-pound bomb, and an auxiliary fuel tank can be seen on each wing of this F-16.

from the mid-1950s gave ground attack planes a new and awesome power. Gradually, with the massive expansion of nuclear forces in the 1960s, the style of war most people imagined began to change. Instead of fighting missile wars with enormously powerful atomic weapons, military planners began to realize that wars fought with conventional, non-nuclear weapons were more likely.

Until the 1970s, The United States Air Force believed it could deter large wars by having nuclear weapons of different types: big ones launched on giant missiles to destroy cities, and small ones dropped by strike planes to stop enemy forces in their tracks. Between the mid-1950s and the end of the 1970s, the air force built a large number of strike planes that could be used to blunt

The F-16 can carry a wide range of rockets, bombs, missiles, and guns.

Some planes, like this British Aerospace Jaguar, are equipped for low-altitude flying and attack targets behind enemy lines.

The air force will equip with nearly 400 F-15E strike planes, one of which is seen here with two special night-sight attack pods.

the sudden attack many people thought likely.

The Soviet Union had built up extremely large forces of men and armaments. Their store of more than 50,000 tanks, guns, and howitzers was far larger than in the West. Instead of trying to match these larger forces, the United States and other European countries sought to use nuclear weapons as a threat to aggression. Military strategists believed the Russians would never dare attack with large forces if they knew they faced a nuclear strike on all fronts.

This view began to change when people realized that if the Russians did attack, and nuclear weapons were used to try and stop them, the countries being defended would themselves be destroyed in the general destruction of nuclear

A single-seat F-16 drops a GBU-16 laser-guided bomb, achieving pinpoint accuracy.

war. It would be like committing suicide. Apart from that, by the 1980s, both the United States and the Soviet Union were making great progress toward reducing nuclear weapons of all types. The West could no longer rely on nuclear forces to deter aggression. That is why the air force today is modernizing its conventional planes. It is trying to find ways to stop aggression through the use of non-nuclear weapons. Ground attack planes carrying conventional weapons are one way to stop armored tank columns.

Close Air Support

Experience with ground attack planes in the Vietnam war showed air force pilots that high-speed fighters converted to carrying bombs and rockets are not as effective as purpose-built planes able to fly slower and lower. Ground attack during the early days of jet planes was typically conducted by a fighter-bomber like the Republic F-84 Thunderjet or Thunderstreak. Later, during the 1960s, the McDonnell Douglas F-4 Phantom II was made to carry bombs and rockets for ground attack. It was a good plane — rugged, well built, and able to hit hard with reasonable accuracy. Yet it left much to be desired because it was essentially a high-speed strike plane designed to fly in fast and get away quick.

What the army wanted from the air force was a plane that could loiter in the sky, hide behind hills and trees, and pop up to attack when it identified an enemy target. The term for this duty was *close air support*. The pilot had to be able to identify the target. Too many fighter-bombers in Vietnam struck the wrong target because the pilots had very little time to identify what it was they were about to hit. Sometimes they hit their own men and machines on the ground. Ground forces thought twice about calling for air support for fear they would be in the line of fire themselves.

There were many design requirements for planes built to do close air support. Agility in the air

Aircraft such as this Soviet MiG-29 pose a significant threat to low-flying strike planes.

was vital. The close air support mission needed planes that could react quickly to the sudden appearance of a ground target, which might be an armored column coming around the bend in a road or a convoy of *armored personnel carriers*. A plane was needed that could find its own target and seek

With the introduction of small nuclear weapons in the 1950s, atomic bombs could be delivered by comparatively small aircraft.

Ground attack means different equipment for different places; in Vietnam, this converted transport Hercules was used to attack communist troops.

Based in Thailand, gun-carrying Hercules transport planes were used against enemy camps hidden in forests or clearings.

out the enemy without waiting for a pre-planned mission to a set target.

It often took too long to request air support and have the planes made ready, fueled and fitted with bombs, then flown out to a target perhaps a hundred miles away. There was also the disadvantage of speed. Too often in Vietnam, the jets saw a target, overshot, and before they could turn back the enemy had scrambled for cover and was nowhere to be seen.

In Vietnam, a wide range of aircraft had been pressed into service. The slow planes were very old and did not have the armament that could hit hard and knock out a target with one shot. Trundling old Dakotas converted into gun platforms bristled with weapons for spraying forests and dense foliage where enemy soldiers were hidden. These planes had anti-personnel weapons but not the performance for maneuverability and tight turns.

Yet the value of air strikes to complement

This F-4E Phantom is carrying a 2,000-pound GBU-10 laser-guided bomb.

ground fighting was demonstrated by one mission in August 1967. With each plane carrying a 3,000-pound bomb, 26 Republic F-105 Thunderchiefs attacked the Paul Doumer bridge carrying road and rail traffic across the Red River at Hanoi. The attack was pressed home in three waves. Each wave had four Phantoms flying top cover against *MiGs* trying to upset the attack and disperse the planes. Four more Phantoms attacked the *anti-aircraft batteries* and four F-105Gs, known as *Wild Weasels,* flew in and jammed the enemy radars.

As bombs were being dropped among the anti-aircraft gunners, the first wave came in at tree-top height, suddenly pulled up to 13,000 feet

Particularly effective during the Vietnam War, the F-105 Thunderchief has a very credible war record.

The Thunderchief was capable of carrying a wide range of weapons for air-to-air and air-to-ground conflict.

and dived straight down at a steep angle toward the bridge. As the bombs were released the air brakes went out and the planes pulled up sharply to get out of the way. One Phantom flew down to 7,000 feet before releasing his bombs and knocked down one of the bridge spans.

By the end of the attack, a railroad and two highway spans had collapsed. It took the Vietnamese nearly two months to repair the

Today, vast numbers of Soviet and East European armored fighting vehicles pose a serious threat to forces in western Europe.

damage, and then the Thunderchiefs came back again and knocked it down. The communists had it working within another month, and the planes returned twice more. After that the Vietnamese left it down for good and built a *pontoon* replacement across the river. Pontoons are small floating barges tied together to provide a makeshift crossing. It crossed the river, but rail traffic was abandoned. With its strikes against targets inside enemy-held territory, the U.S. Air Force helped the army, but could not completely stop the flow of men and materiel. The army still had to fight hard battles, sometimes against heavily armored vehicles. In turn, they needed air cover and planes that could play their part in smashing up enemy tanks and armored vehicles.

From all these hard won lessons, the U.S. Army

An air force F-111 prepares to take off on an attack mission against Libya.

and U.S. Air Force drew up a list of requirements for a special close air support plane that would help ground units defeat enemy armored vehicles. After all the preparations for deterring enemy aggression by stocking up with nuclear weapons, the United States had fought a tough war halfway around the world with conventional weapons and aircraft adapted from other roles. Some of those planes dated back to World War Two. Now, with the lessons learned, it was time to build a special close air support plane that the air force could use to support military ground operations.

Thunderbolt

In March 1967, the U.S. Air Force issued a request to 21 aerospace companies for designs for a special kind of plane. They were looking for one that could maneuver well yet fly in and out of short landing strips, one that had good range and could stay over the target for long periods, and one that could survive intense anti-aircraft fire and not run for cover. Above all, they wanted a plane that could hit tanks with blistering firepower and destroy heavily armored vehicles quickly and completely. Finally, it had to be cheap, reliable, and maintained easily by ground technicians.

On October 10, 1972, prototypes from two companies were brought together for a showdown. One company was Northrop, and the other was Fairchild. Northrop brought a jet-powered plane that looked like a lot of other aircraft. There was nothing particularly different about what they called the A-9. Fairchild, however, showed up with

their A-10. It was very different. From the outset it had the look of a special kind of survivor and was probably the ugliest plane ever built. Pilots would call it the "flying pig," but the air force called it Thunderbolt II.

The A-10 won the competition for the first purpose-built close air support plane. Just as it looked, Thunderbolt II was very different from other aircraft. It was built around the air force requirement for something that could blast tanks, stay airborne amid intense ground fire, and fly home with its pilot alive. To do that it had to be tough, and many aspects of its design had been put there to help it stay in flying condition.

First, the designers gave it what they called a high aspect ratio wing. The *aspect ratio* of a wing is the relative length of the span to the width. A broad wing with a short span is said to have a low aspect

The A-10 Thunderbolt was designed as a rugged ground attack plane based on experience in Vietnam.

The A-10 is designed to carry a powerful gatling gun and a wide variety of bombs and rockets.

To provide protection from ground fire, the two big engines are mounted high up on the rear of the fuselage.

ratio. A wing that has a long span compared to its breadth is said to have a high aspect ratio. Thunderbolt had a high aspect ratio wing to give it good handling and maneuverability at low speeds. It would secure a firm grip on the air when the plane was slowly wheeling and rolling in and out of valleys and threading its way through trees and forests.

Then the designers gave it a twin-fin tail, also to help it stay in the air and carry out extraordinary maneuvers to twist and turn away from enemy fire. The fuselage was basically a flying gun designed around an extremely powerful *gatling-gun* cannon and its enormous ammunition trays. Fuel tanks were wrapped around the top of the fuselage inside the structural frame. They were self-sealing, which means they could take modest amounts of gunfire and not puncture. Thunderbolt carries more than 5 tons of fuel in tanks fitted internally. It can carry external tanks if necessary for ferrying itself from one place to another outside the normal range of the plane.

Two barrel-shaped engine pods are supported at the rear of the fuselage between the wings and the tail, well away from the pilot and his view to either side or down. Set high up on the fuselage, the

The A-10 is designed for ease of maintenance and minimum ground servicing time.

The A-10 pilots sit high on top of the fuselage, directly above the huge gatling gun attached to the nose of the plane.

engines are also in the best position to avoid gunfire from the ground. Each pod contains one General Electric *turbofan engine* that delivers 4.5 tons of thrust. These engines are built for reliability, ruggedness, ease of maintenance, and quiet. Thunderbolt is designed to sneak up on the enemy, not to blast his eardrums with a howling jet *afterburner*!

The plane is built to allow its pilot to look at enemy battle formations from low altitude and then attack selected targets. For a good all-around view, the pilot's cockpit is positioned high up on the forward nose of the fuselage. In this vulnerable position the pilot is exposed to gunfire. To protect

Forward visibility through the bubble-shaped cockpit canopy is good.

him and the mighty cannon which he virtually sits on, engineers have surrounded the area with an armored bath that weighs almost a ton. It has several layers of armor plate and a special foam that helps put out fires, or stop them from starting,

On the ground the aircraft has good clearance, allowing crew members easy access to installation pylons for bombs and rockets.

The A-10 is tough, rugged, and can take a lot of battle damage before it loses the ability to fly.

The A-10 is very maneuverable in the air and can out-turn many fast-flying fighters.

when vital parts are hit by shells. If the pilot has to escape quickly, he does so with his Aces II ejection seat.

To help the plane survive and return from what is perhaps the worst exposure to gunfire, heat, and smoke any aircraft is designed to fly in, special safety features are standard. Apart from armor plate and self-sealing fuel tanks, the fuselage carries two separate sets of flight controls, each with three back-ups. If the hydraulics should be hit

there is a back-up there too. If the back-up gets knocked out, the pilot can use a cable system to work the flying controls.

The flying controls include *ailerons* on the wings, *elevators* on the tail surface, and twin *rudders* on the fins. *Air brakes* are fitted to the outer ailerons so the plane can pull itself up sharp, and *flaps* are carried for general low-speed maneuvering. The undercarriage was made to be simple, although the nose-wheel leg has to be set to one side underneath the fuselage to make room for the gun. Everything on Thunderbolt makes way for the weapons.

Thunderbolt carries basic electronic equipment. It is not supposed to be a sophisticated, highly-advanced aircraft, but rather one that is rugged and survivable, with a powerful punch. To deliver the punch, however, it needs navigation equipment and a weapons delivery system controlled from the cockpit. A special head-up-display, or *HUD*, is attached to the inside of the cockpit above the instrument display in front of the pilot. The HUD gives the pilot important information about the target and the condition of the plane and vital flying information. This data is displayed on a transparent panel which the pilot looks through as he flies the plane. The pilot gets information without having to take his eyes off the view outside for even a second.

Thunderbolts have special sensors that tell them when enemy radar has located the plane. The system is capable of sending out *jamming signals* that turn the enemy radar screen into a fog. There is also a special dispenser for *flares* and *chaff*. Flares are released when enemy *heat-seeking missiles* are launched to home in on the Thunderbolt's hot engines. Forming several different and brighter heat sources, the flares throw the incoming missiles off course and away from the plane. Chaff consists of small metal strips that look like snow on a radar screen, completely hiding the aircraft from view.

Based in England, this A-10 is being loaded with AGM-65 Maverick missiles.

28

Weapons

From the outset, Thunderbolt was built to carry the awesome Avenger gatling gun. The first 21 feet of the plane's 53-foot, 4-inch lower fuselage section is given over completely to the gun and its enormous ammunition tray. The recoil from the gun when it fires is so great that the cannon itself had to be firmly positioned right down the center of the lower fuselage. To make room for the Avenger gun and its equipment, the forward landing gear had to be offset to one side.

General Electric designed the gun and makes it exclusively for the Thunderbolt. There is no other plane in the world today that can carry this fantastic weapon. Nor is there another plane that could use it to such good effect, because the Avenger is specifically designed to be fired from a

The A-10's principal targets are tanks and other armored vehicles, which it is designed to stop with force.

slow, low-flying aircraft. The horsepower generated by the muzzle when the gatling action kicks in is greater than that produced by a German World War Two *King Tiger Tank*.

Avenger is actually seven barrels solidly connected in a group that rotates as the gun fires. Each barrel fires only once before the barrel cluster revolves to the next barrel and fires. Of course, all this happens at tremendous speed, and the rate of fire is controlled by the speed at which the cluster of barrels rotates. The pilot can select two rates of fire — 2,100 rounds per minute or 4,200 rounds per minute. The sheer hitting power of this gun means only very brief bursts of fire are necessary. Two seconds is usually the duration of fire, during which the gun has fired up to 140 *armor-piercing shells*. This amount is equal to more than 200 pounds of ammunition.

Two different types of ammunition can be carried. The armor-piercing incendiary shell is over 6 inches long and more than 1 inch in diameter. This is a lethal charge for hardened tank

Just some of the shells, rockets, bombs, and missiles which the A-10 is capable of carrying on attack missions.

armor and more than sufficient to disable the most heavily protected tank. Depending on the particular type of ammunition carried, between 1,174 and 1,350 rounds can be carried in the ammunition tray and special feed mechanism.

The gun's ammunition is delivered by a hydraulic feed mechanism. The ammunition drum is an enormous, fixed casing directly behind the barrel cluster. The gun weighs just over 2 tons fully loaded with ammunition. The shells alone can weigh 1.5 tons. They are fired toward the target at a speed of more than 2,000 MPH. The hydraulic feed mechanism unloads the gun as well as loading it. If shells are in the barrel at the moment the pilot stops firing, the feeder removes the shells from the gun and returns them to the drum. Within one-half second of pressing the trigger, however, the gun is loaded and firing again.

The giant Avenger gatling gun has seven barrels that rotate at high speed to discharge shells over 6 inches long.

The A-10's gun can fire 70 shells per second, each traveling at a speed of more than 2,000 MPH.

Even equipped with this massive gun, the Thunderbolt can carry a wide range of other weapons for attacking ground targets.

The Thunderbolt relies on more than its Avenger gatling gun for knocking out tanks and heavy skinned armored vehicles. It can carry a maximum 8 tons of weapons on 11 pylons under the fuselage and the wings. These pylons can carry sensor pods to help the plane detect enemy radars that may guide enemy planes to attack it. The plane can drop smoke bombs, jam enemy radars, or carry extra fuel tanks from the pylon positions. Mostly, the pylons are used to carry extra weapons in addition to the Avenger gun, which is standard on every Thunderbolt.

Most of these extra weapons are there to do what the Avenger gun cannot do. One such weapon is the Maverick missile, which is carried in clusters of three. The missile has a small TV camera in its nose and the pilot locks this on to the target before firing the missile. Once fired, the pilot can leave the area and escape, dropping back down to very low altitude to sneak away through the forests and the trees. The missile locks on to the target and accelerates toward it. Maverick has a range of up to 10 miles from low altitude. Planes other than Thunderbolt carry Maverick, and a Maverick missile released from a supersonic strike plane has a range of up to 25 miles.

Another highly effective weapon carried by the Thunderbolt is the Paveway *laser-guided bomb*. The Thunderbolt pilot, another Thunderbolt, or an infantryman on the ground points a low-power laser beam at the target. The laser light is is not strong enough to burn a hole in anything and is invisible to the human eye. The laser light bounces back off the target and is picked up by the Thunderbolt with Paveway. The guided bomb is connected to the reflected laser light and fired. It follows the beam right down to the target, with very great accuracy.

Thunderbolt can carry a wide range of high explosive bombs, fire bombs, practice bombs, TV-guided bombs like Maverick, rockets, missiles,

The high rate of fire can blow apart tank turrets with shells that are easily capable of splitting open the sides of armored vehicles.

The primary operating environment of the A-10 is low down across hilly, wooded land where troops and vehicles are hiding.

and dispensers packed with hundreds of *fragmentation bombs*. These are small bomblets designed to spray out thousands of tiny shrapnel fragments to tear up vehicle tires, tarpaulins, camps, and people. Even extra gun pods can be attached to the pylons. Less powerful than the Avenger, these guns may still come in handy for breaking up less heavily armored units. A main feature of the Thunderbolt is its adaptability to many different duties. With the diverse and broad range of weapons, pods, and fuel tanks it is equipped to carry, the plane can carry out numerous operational responsibilities. Always, first and foremost, it is a tank buster.

Parachutes reduce the speed of falling bombs, allowing the slow-moving Thunderbolt to be out of harm's way when they explode.

Thunderbolt pilots sight their weapons through a special aiming device on the front windscreen.

On Patrol

When Thunderbolt was first designed it competed against a Northrop air support plane, but there was really no competition at all. Thunderbolt was just what the air force wanted, and it moved into production during 1973. The air force received its first operational Thunderbolt in November 1975. Six months later the first unit became ready for action at Davis-Monthan Air Force Base in Arizona. At the end of 1977, Thunderbolts flew simulated combat missions against U.S. Air Force planes pretending to be Soviet fighters. They came from the 64th Aggressor Squadron to test the plane against possible threats they might face in war.

Because the plane is built for rugged, survivable operations in the toughest battle conditions, it was necessary to prove just how tough it was. To do that, one Thunderbolt was pumped full of high-explosive incendiary shells, armor-piercing shells and other small-*caliber* rounds. In all, the aircraft was hit with more than 800 rounds, 430 going into the cockpit armor, 172 into the wings, 58 rounds into the gun ammunition tray, 108 into the fuselage and tail, 23 into bomb pylons under the wings, and 24 into the windshield panels. The plane survived.

The first operational Thunderbolt squadron in Europe was the 92nd Tactical Fighter Squadron of the 81st Tactical Fighter Wing. It arrived at Bentwaters, England, in 1979 and built up to a strength of 108 Thunderbolts, replacing the F-4D Phantoms that had been assigned a close air support role. Various exercises were carried out in Europe, including "Dawn Patrol" in Aviano, Italy.

When a target is located, individual planes peel off and attack one by one.

Although A-10s usually fly in units, they do not generally stay so close together.

Exercises like this were flown against other *U.S.A.F.* aircraft simulating Soviet fighters. Northrop F-5 aircraft are used to play the Soviet role.

A-10 units would be prime targets for enemy interceptors out to stop the attack planes getting through.

Big and chunky, Thunderbolt is surprisingly docile to fly. Its big wing, 57 feet, 6 inches across, gives it plenty of grip on the air. Its fuselage is 53 feet, 4 inches long and the plane stands 14 feet, 8 inches high on the ground. Maximum operating weight is 21 tons, of which 8 tons can be armament in addition to the Avenger gatling gun. The plane can carry extra fuel in tanks attached to the wing

A-10s drop 500-pound bombs on a ground target.

There is little protection from the awesome fire power of an aggressive A-10 delivering its warload.

pylons, and this enables it to ferry itself long distances.

A typical ferry flight gets the maximum possible efficiency from the plane and its extra fuel load. The ferry flight would begin at a height of 25,000 feet and a speed of 304 knots. As the flight progresses and the plane gets lighter, altitude gradually increases to 35,000 feet and speed drops off to 286 knots. With 20 minutes reserve flying time left, the Thunderbolt can fly almost 2,600 miles non-stop. This gives it good opportunity to fly from one country to another without relying on big cargo planes or in-flight tanker planes. If Thunderbolt has to fly longer distances, however, it can refill its tanks in flight from aerial tankers.

The two types of combat mission ground attack planes fly are battlefield air support and close air support (CAS). The battlefield mission is typical for an attack on enemy armor and fixed installations. Thunderbolt would fly at a height of 5,000 feet 250 miles to its target, spend 30 minutes over the attack zone at very low level, and return back to base, again at 5,000 feet. The CAS mission would begin with the Thunderbolt flying out at 25,000 feet before dropping to low level. Once there it can throttle back on one engine and spend almost two hours loitering and looking for targets. Or it can go in with guns blazing for a short, sharp, 10-minute combat. On the way back in friendly airspace it cruises home at 35,000 feet.

The U.S. Air Force has about 650 Thunderbolts, of which 460 are in operational service. The rest are in training or reserve units but could be called upon in time of crisis. Thunderbolt is undoubtedly a unique plane, yet its design is now about 20 years old, and plans are being made to design its replacement. When Thunderbolt is eventually replaced, it will go into the history books as being the first aircraft designed purposely for close air support.

A-10 Thunderbolts can re-fuel in mid-air to extend their range and operating radius.

Big Punch

The need for the Thunderbolt was first really defined by experience in Vietnam. Its role was shaped by the belief that massive Soviet tank columns would pose a serious threat in wartime. Thunderbolt enables the U.S. Air Force to do many jobs in support of operations on the ground. Yet, for all its adaptability, it is relatively slow and does not have great range. The big punch that comes from high-speed strike planes flying deep into enemy-held territory with powerful conventional or nuclear weapons is provided by other warplanes.

The most commonly used U.S.A.F. tactical strike planes today are the General Dynamics F-111E and F models. Both are developments of the F-111 fighter, originally designed to provide both air force and navy with a replacement for older fighters. The F-111 first flew in December 1964. The plane never did make it into navy service, and the air force used it in Vietnam with mixed results. Now, it has big responsibilities in the attack role. With a maximum weight of around 47 tons, the plane is heavy, but it can carry 2 tons inside its bomb bay and up to 6.5 tons on wing pylons.

A single F-111F strike plane battles through heavy weather with twelve Mark-82 bombs.

The F-111E/F has a top speed of around 800 MPH at very low altitude or 1,400 MPH at high altitude. It has a range of 3,000 miles on internal fuel, which means it can strike targets 1,500 miles from base and get back without aerial refueling. The F-111E/F has been around a long time, and one other version is used as a long-range strategic bomber carrying several nuclear weapons. The

Using a special laser sighting device, this F-111F carries four Mark-84 laser-guided bombs.

Developed specifically for the ground attack role, the F-15E is a further development of the Eagle, a formidable strike plane capable of attacking ground targets in all weather conditions.

The F-15 Eagle all-weather air-superiority fighter is equally at home carrying a heavy warload of bombs.

strike version of the F-111 is on the margin of what could reasonably be accepted as a ground attack plane.

Much more like the traditional ground attack plane is the strike version of the famous McDonnell Douglas F-15 Eagle. Known as the F-15E, this plane is a development of the Eagle *air superiority fighter.* An air superiority fighter is one designed to seize control of the air and keep it. To do that it must be rugged, able to carry a wide range of weapons, and fly far and fast. The Eagle is capable of 1,600 MPH high up and can carry 11.75 tons of bombs, rockets, or missiles in clusters up to a maximum 26 of any one type. It comes with a standard 20mm General Electric M61 Vulcan

Britain, West Germany, and Italy operate Tornado strike planes to support U.S. Air Force strike missions in Europe.

gatling gun for use against ground targets or other planes.

Because the F-15 was designed primarily as a fighter, it has all of the basic characteristics of an aircraft built for the air combat role. When its day's work as a strike plane is done and its weapons have been released, it is free to fly and fight an aerial war. It can shoot its way out of a scrap with other planes or go after enemy fighters attacking friendly

aircraft. It has good range and is a robust warplane built to operate in the world's worst weather conditions.

The F-15 has two crew members sitting high on top the wedge-shaped fuselage, which is 63 feet, 9 inches long. The wing spans 42 feet, 10 inches across, and the twin tail fins give the heavy plane good handling characteristics. At maximum, the F-15 weighs 40 tons with a full load of ammunition and weapons. The F-15 is given the job of trying to stop enemy forces by using conventional weapons rather than relying on a wave of nuclear bombs. It is part of the new strategy to meet the enemy on the battlefield with non-nuclear weapons. The air force expects to buy nearly 400 F-15s.

This Tornado attack plane carries a special pod under the fuselage capable of releasing thousands of bomblets to smash up concrete runways.

The F-15 has a big part to play because it is one of the most capable, all-weather strike planes around. Britain, Italy, and West Germany operate another very capable strike plane. Called the Tornado, it was built by a team put together from the three countries. The Tornado is rugged and has enormous hitting power with a long range and special radar to help it fly very fast close to the ground. It is one of the new generation of warplanes built to assist the troops on the ground in the ground attack role.

GLOSSARY

Afterburner	A pipe at the back of the jet engine where additional fuel is added to exhaust gases, causing them to re-ignite. This process gives the aircraft much greater thrust for short periods.
Aileron	The flying surfaces usually attached to the outer sections of an aircraft wing and used for lateral (roll) control.
Air brakes	Large door-like surfaces designed to extend outward into the flow of air and give the plane greater drag, thereby slowing it up in the air.
Air superiority fighter	An aircraft built to gain control of the skies over friendly or unfriendly territory by attacking and destroying enemy aircraft in the air.
Anti-aircraft batteries	Groups of anti-aircraft guns or guided missiles.
Armor-piercing shells	Fired from an aircraft gun, these shells are designed to penetrate protective armor attached to tanks or armored personnel carriers.
Armored personnel carriers	Tracked or wheeled vehicles protected with armor plate and used to carry infantry men.
Aspect ratio	The length of an airplane's wing compared to its width. A wing with a long span compared to its width is said to have a high aspect ratio. A broad wing with a short span has a low aspect ratio.
Blitzkrieg	The German word for lightning war, the name given to surprise attack involving ground attack planes and tanks.
Caliber	The internal diameter of a gun barrel, usually used to express its power.
Chaff	Small metal strips that look like snow on a radar screen and completely hide the aircraft from view.
Close air support	The use of aircraft to attack ground targets in support of surface operations.
Elevators	Control surfaces carried on the horizontal section of an aircraft tail and generally used for pitch (up and down) control.
Flaps	Large panels usually carried on the rear surfaces of an aircraft wing. When lowered, they give the aircraft additional lift at low speed.
Flares	Bright sources of heat similar to firecrackers. When ejected from an aircraft, flares attract heat-seeking missiles and throw them off course.
Fragmentation bombs	Small bombs designed to spray out thousands of tiny shrapnel fragments.
Gatling gun	A type of gun in which several barrels are positioned together in a cluster. As a barrel fires, the cluster rotates into position for the next barrel. This action continues while the gun is being used.
Head-Up Display (HUD)	A device that projects vital flight information onto a transparent panel in front of the windscreen, enabling the pilot to read critical measurements without taking his eyes off the view ahead.

46

Heat-seeking missiles	Missiles with small infra-red devices designed to lock onto the hot exhaust of an aircraft engine.
Interceptors	Fighter planes designed to attack approaching enemy aircraft.
Jamming signals	Electronic signals sent out by an aircraft or by a ground device to jam the radio or radar equipment of an enemy aircraft or ground unit.
King Tiger Tank	The largest and most powerful tank operated by the German army during World War Two. It weighed 50 tons and carried heavy armor plate as protection.
Laser-guided bomb	A bomb that locks onto a target reflected by a laser light invisible to the human eye. The laser can be transmitted either from the aircraft that launched the missile, from a second laser device on the ground, or from another aircraft.
MiG	The name applied to the leading Soviet fighter and attack planes. MiG is an abbreviation for Mikoyan Gurevich, the Soviet aircraft factory that makes the planes.
Pontoon	Small floating barges tied together to provide a make-shift bridge.
Rudders	The vertical tail surfaces that move to give the aircraft directional (left and right) control.
Turbofan engine	A jet engine with blades arranged in a circle like a fan to increase the amount of air delivered to the combustion chamber.
Wild Weasel	The name given to an aircraft fitted for electronic jamming of enemy radar. Wild Weasels provide a screen through which friendly fighters can safely penetrate enemy air space.

INDEX

Page references in *italics* indicate photographs or illustrations.